Enjoy Your Homestay

I Talk You Talk Press

Copyright © 2018 I Talk You Talk Press

ISBN: 978-4-909733-18-4

www.italkyoutalk.com

info@italkyoutalk.com

All rights reserved. No part of this publication may be resold, reproduced, stored in retrieval system, copied in any form or by any means, electronic, mechanical, photocopying, recording or otherwise transmitted without the prior written permission from the publisher. You must not circulate this publication in any format, online or otherwise.

This is a work of fiction. Names, characters, businesses, organizations, products, places, events and incidents are either the products of the author's imagination or are used in a fictitious manner. We have no affiliation with any existing companies mentioned in this story. Any resemblance to actual persons, living or dead, existing stories or actual events is purely coincidental.

Although the author and publisher have made every effort to ensure that the contents of this book were correct at press time, the author and publisher do not assume and hereby disclaim any liability to any party for any loss, damage, or disruption caused by errors or omissions, whether such errors or omissions result from negligence, accident, or any other cause.

For more information, see the Copyright Notice on our website.

Image copyright: © jedi-master - Fotolia.com #28485871 Standard License

CONTENTS

Introduction	1
Format of this book	4
1. Before you go	5
2. Take some conversation with you!	7
3. Meeting the host family	9
COFFEE BREAK	12
4. Manners	13
5. Arriving at your homestay house	15
6. The first day	18
COFFEE BREAK	21
7. The bathroom	22
8. The laundry	24
9. Eating	26

COFFEE BREAK	31
10. Daily conversation	32
11. Instructions and directions	34
12. Presents	36
COFFEE BREAK	37
13. Sickness and accidents	38
14. Saying goodbye	40
Thank You	42
About the Author	44

INTRODUCTION

So, you are going on a homestay! Of course, you must be very excited.

You will have the chance to experience real daily life in another country, and practice your English.

You will have the chance to make new friends, and to learn about their culture. It will be a great experience, which you will never forget!

But perhaps you are also a little nervous. Perhaps you are worried about communicating with your host family. Will you be able to express yourself? Will you be able to communicate smoothly? If you are worried about these things, this book is for you.

In this book we give you advice, and many example sentences and conversations, to help you communicate.

We have been teaching English for many years. A lot of our students have enjoyed the great experience of staying with a family in another country. When the students return to us, we ask them about their experiences. We also talk to host families.

Why do we do this?

The answer is that we want to know how to help our students prepare for their homestay. We want our students to have the best time possible. We want the host families to have a great experience too.

Remember, the homestay is also a cultural experience for the host family. It might be their first time to host a student, or it might be their first time to host a student from your country. In any case, it is their first time to host you! They may be nervous, just like you. They want you to have a nice time, and to enjoy your stay with them.

Many students come back from their homestay satisfied and happy, and many host families have a good time too. But not all. Some students come back disappointed. Some hosts also feel the homestay was not successful.

Over the years we have gathered many comments from host families and from students. On the following pages you can read some of the comments. Read the comments and think about the problem in each case.

Some Student Comments

1) *"The host family didn't talk to me."*
2) *"I didn't know what to say."*
3) *"I didn't like the food."*
4) *"I stayed with the host family for a month and there was never any rice. I missed eating rice."*
5) *"I was very interested in the food. I wanted to learn how to cook some western style recipes. The host mother was often busy in the kitchen. She never asked me to join her."*
6) *"I wanted to help in the house, but I didn't know what to do. I was worried I would do something wrong."*
7) *"I wanted to do things with the family, but they never invited me to join them."*

Some Host Family Comments

1) *"He was so quiet. It seemed he didn't want to talk to us."*
2) *"We tried to talk to our homestay guest. Our guest only said 'yes' or 'no'. We could ask questions and receive an answer, but we couldn't have a conversation."*
3) *"I asked our homestay guest what she liked to eat. She said anything was OK. But she didn't eat very much. I tried different styles of food. I asked her if she liked the meals. She always said 'yes', but I don't think she liked my cooking."*
4) *"I asked him what food he would like to eat. He said he wanted to eat local specialties. Some of our local specialties are very expensive but I tried hard to give him the food he wanted. We usually eat Asian style once or twice a week. But while our guest was with us, I only cooked western style food."*
5) *"I love to cook. I thought I could cook meals with my homestay guest. She*

could teach me how to cook her style of food and I could show her how to make some western style dishes. But she never came into the kitchen. She sat at the dining table and waited for me to serve food to her."

6) *"She didn't do anything in the house. She didn't offer to help with washing dishes or clearing the table."*

7) *"Our children were excited when our international guest arrived. They wanted to play with him. They wanted to show him their school. They thought he would go to watch them play sport on Saturdays. But he never spoke to them. He didn't seem to be interested in the children's lives."*

Why do these things happen?
Cultural differences can cause problems and misunderstandings.

A homestay is a chance for you and your host family to understand new cultures. Another reason to go on a homestay is to practice your English.

So how can we make sure that everyone has a great homestay experience?
Good communication!

All of the problems above could be solved if everyone communicated well.

This book gives you advice on how to overcome communication difficulties and cultural differences.

We give you ideas, words and phrases, so you always have something to say.

If you practice hard, you will be able to have a conversation, give an opinion, talk about new ideas, and talk about things that are a problem for you.

FORMAT OF THIS BOOK

Each unit starts with a question and an answer section. The questions are real questions from students going on homestays.

The next section has sample sentences and sample conversations to give you the tools you need to communicate smoothly.

There are also "coffee break" columns, with real life stories from teachers, host families and students.

We hope this book is useful to you, and we hope you have a wonderful homestay!

1. BEFORE YOU GO

Q: Should I contact the host family before I go?
Advice: Yes.
There are five good reasons.
1) It is polite.
2) The host family will be wondering about you. Who are you? What are you like? What do you like?
3) It makes you feel less nervous. You will "break the ice". ("Break the ice" means "get to know someone".)
4) You have the chance to ask questions.
5) You can tell your host family about any allergies you have, or if there is any food that you don't eat.*

* Maybe you arranged your homestay through an agency. Maybe you filled out a form that asked you about allergies and food preferences. If you did this, it is not necessary to put it in your message to your host family.

Example email
---Dear Mr and Mrs Smith,
My name is Satoshi Nakata. I will be staying with you for two weeks. I will arrive next Wednesday. It is my first time to leave Japan, and I am very excited, but a little nervous.
I'd like to tell you a little about myself. I am 19 years old, and I live in Chiba Prefecture, near Tokyo. I study economics at university. There are 4 people in my family - my father, mother, younger brother and me. In my free time, I enjoy reading and listening to music. I often go to rock concerts. I also like winter sports.

I go skiing and snowboarding every winter.

I'd like you to know that I have an allergy to dairy products like cheese, yoghurt and milk. I become ill if I eat any of these, so I must be careful. I also have an allergy to dogs. I hope my allergies will not cause problems for you.

I'm looking forward to meeting you next week.

Best regards,

Satoshi Nakata---

2. TAKE SOME CONVERSATION WITH YOU!

Q: I'm nervous about communicating in English. What can I talk about with my host family?

Advice: If you feel nervous about communicating in English with your host family, take some conversation with you!

It is a good idea to have some photographs of your family, home and hometown. You could have photographs on your mobile phone or some printed photographs. Practice talking about the photographs. Your host family will be interested in your life, your family, and the way you live.

Example Sentences:

1) I have an older brother and a younger sister. Our grandmother lives with us. Here is a photograph of all the family.

2) This is a photograph of my sister in kimono. We have a ceremony called "Coming of Age". All the 20-year-olds dress in kimono for the ceremony.

3) I have two daughters and two grandchildren. This is a photograph of all the family. It was taken at my nephew's wedding.

4) This is my home. It was built about eighty years ago. It is in the middle of town.

5) My hometown is very small. There are only about 5,000 people living there. It is famous for violin-making and strawberries.

Think about your life. Write down some sentences about yourself and practice them.

More Example Sentences:

6) I worked in a bank for thirty years. When I retired, I decided to learn to speak English well.

7) I am a medical student. My father is a doctor too. When I graduate, I hope to work in a big city hospital for a few years.

8) On weekends, my friends and I like to go to the city. We enjoy shopping.

3. MEETING THE HOST FAMILY

Q. What should I call my hosts when I meet them? I heard that people in English-speaking countries use first names. My host father is called John Smith and my host mother is called Diana Smith. Should I call them John and Diana? Or should I call them Mr and Mrs Smith?

Advice: When you meet the host family for the first time, call them Mr Smith and Mrs Smith.

Smith is the "last name" or "surname" or "family name". John and Diana are the "first names" or "given names". It is very likely that they will say "please call me (first name)", but until they do, use formal English - Mr and Mrs + "last name".

Many students think that people in English speaking countries use first names only, but this is not true. It depends on the situation. If you are a school student, you never call a teacher by his or her first name, unless the teacher tells you to. If you don't know a person well, you should use Mr/Ms + "last name" until the person says "please call me (first name)." Then, it is OK to use first names. (You can use children's first names from the beginning.)

The host family might also be wondering what to call you, so tell them the name you prefer.

Example Sentence:
My name is Satoshi Nakata. Please call me Satoshi.

Example Conversations at the Airport:
1)
Host: Welcome Satoshi! I'm John Smith. How do you do?*
Satoshi: Nice to meet you, Mr Smith.
Host: Please call me John.
Satoshi: OK, thank you John.

2)
Host: Hi Satoshi. I'm Diana Smith. Call me Diana.
Satoshi: Nice to meet you, Diana.

Be careful! *How do you do?
"How do you do" does not mean "How are you?" It means "Nice to meet you". It is not a question!

Q: Should I shake hands?
Advice: Yes, with your right hand. This is a normal custom, especially for men. When you shake hands, grip the other person's hand firmly (but not too firmly!) Many women shake hands too.

Q: What can I say about my trip?
Advice: Your hosts will probably ask you about your trip. How do you answer? Let's look at some examples.

Example Conversations:
1)
John: Did you have a good trip?
Satoshi: Yes, thank you.

This is **not** a good answer because it stops the communication. It seems like Satoshi does not want to have a conversation. It is better to add some extra information. If you just say 'yes' or 'no', your host family may worry that you are sick, or you didn't have a good trip. Even if your English level is low, you can still add a little extra information.

Your target in the beginning should be Answer +.

When you feel more confident, make your target Answer ++.

2)
John: Did you have a good trip? / How was your trip?

Satoshi: Yes, it was great. I really enjoyed it. I watched movies on the plane and slept for a few hours.

OR

It was very long. I left my home 30 hours ago, but I slept a little on the plane.

OR

It was OK, but I'm a little tired now. I'm sure I will sleep well tonight!

Q. What can I say if I feel unwell after the flight, or if I need to go to the toilet?

Advice: Tell your hosts. Don't try to wait until you get to their home!

Example Sentences:

1) I'm sorry, I need to use the bathroom / go to the toilet / go to the restroom.

2) I think I am going to be sick*. Could you find somewhere to stop the car please?

*to be sick means "to vomit"

COFFEE BREAK

"When I visit new countries, I love to go to supermarkets. It is so interesting to see the different food. I asked my host family if I could go to the supermarket with them sometime. I enjoyed it a lot. I planned to take gifts back for my co-workers and friends. I thought I would buy cookies and chocolates. My host family said, 'Look in the supermarket. If you can find the gifts you want, they will be much cheaper. The airport gift shops are expensive.' My host family was right. I bought most of my gifts in the local supermarket."
Ms T.K. (26) Visited Australia

"My host family had three children. The children played sport every Saturday. I asked if I could go to watch. I went to a children's football match. The club was raising money. They were cooking sausages and selling them. I asked if I could help. I was in charge of ketchup and bread. I had a lot of fun and I spoke to many people."
Mr M.O (19) Visited New Zealand

4. MANNERS

Q. I am going on a homestay to an English-speaking country. The culture is very different to mine. I don't want to do or say anything rude. Can you give me some advice?

Advice: Basic manners are very important, but very easy. So you do not need to worry so much. If you follow these basic points, you will be fine.

Point 1: Please and thank you.

This is very important, but surprisingly, some homestay families tell us that the student staying with them did not say please or thank you. Perhaps they felt shy or perhaps they forgot. If you ask someone for something, or to do something for you, don't forget to add please. If someone does something for you, or gives you something, say thank you. When you refuse something, for example, your host mother asks, "Do you want a cup of tea?" Don't just answer "no". Say "No thank you", or "No thank you, not at the moment" or "No thank you, I had a drink before I left the language school".

This may seem like simple, basic advice, but it is surprising how many people forget these simple words when they are communicating in a foreign language.

Point 2: Make eye contact when you speak.

In English-speaking countries, it is normal to look at the other person while speaking. Of course, you should not stare at the other person, or look at them all the time, but when you are telling someone something, or asking something, it is normal and polite to look at the other person. If you don't, it can look rude, or it can look like you cannot be trusted. Sometimes people think that no eye contact means that the speaker doesn't like them.

Point 3: Excuse me and sorry.

If you need to speak to someone, but they are speaking to someone else, you should wait for them to finish. If you cannot wait, you should say "Excuse me, I'm sorry to interrupt, but…."

If you do something wrong, say "I'm sorry." If you can, try to offer to make things better. For example, "I'm sorry but I dropped a glass and it broke. Shall I buy you a new one?"

These simple words, **please, thank you, sorry, excuse me,** and also eye contact are enough to show your good manners.

And don't forget to smile!

5. ARRIVING AT YOUR HOMESTAY HOUSE

Q. What can I say when we arrive at the house?
Advice: Many people work hard to keep their houses and gardens looking nice. You should try to say some positive things about the house and garden.

Example Sentences:
1) You have a very nice house. I live in an apartment, so it seems very big to me.
2) Your garden is beautiful. I like the flowers. It is much bigger than our garden.
3) We don't have a garden.
4) We have a big garden because I live on a farm, but our garden is different from this.
5) Do you grow vegetables? How much time do you spend gardening?

Q. Should I take my shoes off?
Advice: Check with your host family. Some people wear shoes in the house, but others don't. In English-speaking countries, there is no clear rule. Each family will have their own culture. In New Zealand for example, if you take your shoes off, you should put them in your room, not leave them at the door. But other families will wear business shoes in the house but keep sports shoes and garden shoes in a room behind the kitchen.

Watch and see what the family does. Or be brave and ask!

Example Sentences:
1) Should I take my shoes off?
2) Do you wear shoes in the house?
3) Where should I leave my shoes?
4) In my country, we always take our shoes off and leave them next to the front door. What do you do?

Example Conversation:
Satoshi: Your garden is beautiful. I like the flowers.
John: Thank you. We enjoy gardening. Do you have a garden?
Satoshi: No, I live in an apartment. Do you wear shoes in the house?
John: No we don't. We take them off at the front door and put them in our rooms.
Satoshi: Oh, I see.

Q. Should I make a comment about my room when I see it for the first time?

Advice: When your host family takes you to your room, it is polite to say something nice about it. If you don't, your host family may be worried that you don't like the room.

Example Sentences:
1) This is a very nice room. I like it. Thank you.
2) This is a very nice room. I will enjoy staying here.
3) How nice!
4) Oh! I have a desk! That will be very useful, because I have to study.

If the room has a nice view, you can say, "The view is wonderful!"
If you are not sure where to put your things, you can ask questions like
Where should I hang my clothes?
Where should I leave my shoes?

Q. Will my host family clean my room?

Advice: You should keep your room clean and tidy. Make your bed every day. Put your clothes away in the closet and put your shoes in the closet or under your bed. Keep your laundry together in a bag.

6. THE FIRST DAY

Q. If I feel very tired when I arrive at the host family's house, is it OK to rest? Or should I stay awake and talk? Is it rude to go to sleep?

Advice: If you have been travelling for a long time, you will probably be tired. Your host family will understand this, and they will expect you to be tired!

Example Sentences:
1) I feel a little tired. Do you mind if I take a nap*?
2) I feel sleepy. Is it OK if I rest for a while?
3) I want to adjust to the time difference.
4) I think I have jet lag.
5) What time should I wake up?

A nap is a short sleep.

Example Conversation:
Satoshi: I feel a little tired. Do you mind if I take a nap?
Diane: No, not at all. I'm sure you are very tired.
Satoshi: Thank you. What time should I wake up?
Diane: We will have dinner around 6:30.
Satoshi: OK, could you wake me up before then, please? OR OK, I'll set my alarm clock.

Your host family might ask you if you want something to eat or drink.

Example Conversations:
1)
Diane: Would you like something to eat before you rest?
Satoshi: No, I'm fine, thank you, but could I have something to drink?
Diane: What would you like?
Satoshi: Could I have a glass of water please?
Diane: Sure.

2)
Diane: Are you hungry?
Satoshi: Yes, I'm a little hungry.
Diane: How about a sandwich?
Satoshi: That sounds nice, thank you.

3)
Diane: Did you sleep well?
Satoshi: Yes, I slept very well thank you. OR I had a good rest.

Q. I promised my family I would send them a message when I arrived. How can I ask about sending a message?
Advice: Most homes will have an Internet connection. Remember international phone calls might be expensive, so if your family has Internet, an email is the easiest and cheapest way to contact your family.

Example Sentences:
1) I'm sorry to ask, but do you have an Internet connection / WIFI?
2) My family will want to get a message from me.
3) May I use your computer to send a short message to my family?
4) Could you connect me to the Internet?"
5) I must send a short message to my family.

Example Conversation:
Satoshi: I don't want to trouble you, but I am the first person from my family to travel to another country. My family is a little

worried. Could I send them a message to say I arrived safely, and I am very happy?

John: Sure. Would you like to telephone them?

Satoshi: No thank you. I am sure international calls are expensive. A short email will be fine.

John: OK. I will help you. Do you have a Yahoo account?

Satoshi: I use Gmail.

John: No problem. The computer is in the family room. I will show you.

Satoshi: Thank you very much.

Be careful!

Never use the host family's computer without asking.

Remember the host family might need their computer for work or study. Even if your hosts invite you to use their computer, remember Internet connections in some countries are very expensive. If it is used a lot, the family might have to pay a lot of money.

COFFEE BREAK

"Our children play basketball. We have a basketball hoop outside. The children use it for practice. When Marco was staying with us, he often joined the children. He was a good player and taught them some new skills. It was very nice for all of us. The children loved him, and they were very sad when he returned to Italy."

Host mother to a student from Italy

"We often have international visitors as homestay guests. The guests often bring small gifts. One of the best gifts was a packet of origami paper and a little book about paper folding. Hana showed our children how to make paper birds. The children were pleased. They took their paper birds to school to show their teacher."

Host mother to a student from Japan

7. THE BATHROOM

Q. Should I take a shower in the morning, or can I have a bath at night?

Advice: It depends on the family. Some bathrooms only have a shower, some only have a bath, some have both. Some people take a shower in the morning before they go to school or work. Some people take a shower or bath at night, when they get home. Some people do both. You should check when it is OK to have a shower or bath.

In some countries, and some houses, there might be a limited amount of hot water. If so, you shouldn't use too much.

Example Sentences:
1) I usually take a bath at night. Will that be OK?
2) What time is it OK for me to use the bathroom?
3) What is the best time for me to have a shower?
4) Where should I put my wet towel?
5) Where should I leave my soap / wash bag / shampoo?

The shower or hot water system might be different from the system in your home country. If you don't know how to use it, ask.

Example Sentences:
1) Could you show me how to turn on the shower?
2) There is no hot water. Could you show me what to do?

Example Conversation:
Satoshi: Could you show me how to turn on the shower?
Diane: Sure. Press this switch here, and then turn this. It takes a few seconds for the water to become warm. When you have finished, just press this switch here.

8. THE LAUNDRY

Q: Will my host family wash my clothes, or should I wash them myself?
Advice: It depends on the host family. Some families might wash all your clothes. Other families might expect you to wash your own clothes.

Example Sentences:
1) I need to wash some clothes.
2) Could I use the washing machine please?
3) Could you show me how to use the washing machine please?
4) I have some clothes to hand wash. Where can I wash them?
5) Where should I hang my laundry/washing?
6) Should I use the clothes dryer?
7) May I use the clothes dryer?
8) Do you have an iron I could borrow?

Example Conversations:
1)
Satoshi: I need to wash some clothes. Could I use the washing machine please?
Diane: Of course. Do you have a lot to wash?
Satoshi: Just a few things.
Diane: Come into the laundry and I'll show you. This is the washing machine. And this is the dryer. It is going to rain today, so you can't hang your clothes outside.

Satoshi: Could you show me how to use the washing machine please?

Diane: Sure. This is the soap powder. Put it in here, then press this button, and then press start.

Satoshi: Thank you. I'll get my clothes.

2)
Satoshi: I need to wash some clothes. Could I use the washing machine please?

Diane: Don't worry. Just put your laundry on top of the washing machine and I will do it with the family's laundry.

3)
Satoshi: Do you have an iron I could borrow?
Diane: Yes, of course. I'll go and get it for you.
Satoshi: Thank you.

9. EATING

Q. Will my host family prepare all my meals?
Advice: It depends on the homestay conditions, but most homestays provide breakfast and dinner. Some may prepare a lunch box for you. Or, you may have to buy your lunch yourself. If you are going out at night, and do not need an evening meal, make sure you tell your host family so they don't prepare one for you. Always give a reason too. If you just say "I don't need dinner tonight", it sounds rude.

Example Sentences:
1) There is a party at the language school tonight, so I don't need any dinner.
2) I am going out for dinner with my friends tonight.
3) I am going to buy lunch at the cafeteria tomorrow, so I don't need a lunch box.
4) We are going on a trip today and we will have lunch in a restaurant, so I don't need a lunch box.

Example Conversation:
Satoshi: I am going out with some new friends from the language school tonight, so I don't need dinner.
Diane: Oh, I see. Thank you for telling me. What time will you come back?
Satoshi: I don't know. Maybe around 9 o'clock.
Diane: OK. Call if you have any problems. I hope you have a

great time.
Satoshi: Thank you.

Q. What kind of food will my host family serve?

Advice: It depends on the country and the host family's culture. Breakfast will probably be simple – fruit juice, milk, tea, coffee, bread, toast, jam, honey, peanut butter, cereal, fruit. Your host family might make breakfast for you, or they might tell you to prepare your own, or to help yourself.

Lunch may be a lunch box called a "packed lunch". The packed lunch might have sandwiches, fruit, meat, fish, vegetables or snacks, such as crisps/potato chips, or chocolate. There might be rice instead of sandwiches. It depends on the family.

Dinner could be anything – meat, fish, pasta, pizza, curry, vegetables…

So, make sure you tell your host family if there is any food you don't like.

Example Sentences:
1) I'm vegetarian
2) I'm vegan
3) I cannot eat fish/seafood
4) I cannot eat meat/pork
5) I have a peanut allergy
6) I am allergic to wheat/eggs
7) I cannot have dairy products/milk/animal products

Example Conversations:
1)
Diane: Is there any food you don't like?
Satoshi: I like most kinds of food, but I cannot eat dairy products like cheese, yoghurt or milk.
Diane: Oh yes. You told me that in your email.
John: Are you allergic to them?
Satoshi: Yes, I am.
Diane: Are eggs OK?
Satoshi: Yes, eggs are fine.

2)

Diane: What do you usually have for breakfast?

Satoshi: I usually have rice, fish and miso soup, but I will eat the same breakfast as you. What do you have?

Diane: We have egg and toast, and fruit juice and coffee or tea. Is that OK for you?

Satoshi: It sounds great, thank you.

3)
Diane: I'll make you a packed lunch every day. Are ham salad sandwiches OK?

Satoshi: That sounds good, thank you.

Q. What should I do if I don't like some of the food the host family makes?

Advice: One of the fun parts of going on a homestay or visiting another country is trying new food. You don't have to eat food you don't like, but it is polite to try a little before you decide you don't like it! Also, how you say you don't like it and don't want any more is important.

Example Sentences:
1) I've never had that before. What is it?
2) I'd like to try a little.
3) It tastes very good. May I have some more?
4) I'm sorry. The taste is a little strange / too strong for me. I don't really like it.
5) I don't usually eat this kind of food.
6) I like it, but I don't think I want to eat any more.

Example Conversations:
1)
Diane: Have you had Shepherd's Pie before?

Satoshi: No, I haven't. What is it?

Diane: It is meat, with carrots and onions, topped with mashed potato.

Satoshi: It sounds nice. I'd like to try a little.

2)
Satoshi: It's very good. May I have some more?

Diane: I'm glad you like it. Help yourself.
Satoshi: Thank you.

3)
Satoshi: I'm sorry. The taste is a little strong for me. I don't really like it.
Diane: That's OK. Have some more salad instead.

Q. What should I say if I get too much food and I can't finish it? Or too little food?
Advice: Use the polite phrases below to tell your host family.

Example Sentences:
1) I'm sorry. The meal is really nice, but I'm not used to eating so much.
2) I don't usually eat so much cheese/meat.
3) I'm sorry. I don't think I can finish my meal. I'm very full.
4) I think it was a bit too much for me.
5) I am really hungry today. Could I have a little more? It is really delicious.

Q. What should I say when I finish eating? Is just "thank you" OK?
Advice: It is polite to say something about the meal.

Example Sentences:
1) Thank you. That was wonderful.
2) Thank you. That was really delicious.
3) Thank you. I really enjoyed that.
4) That was a very nice meal. Thank you.

Q. Should I offer to help clean up after the meal?
Advice: It is polite to offer. Your host family may see you as a guest, or they may see you as a member of the family and expect you to do your share of the housework. Helping is also a good opportunity to learn new ways of doing things, and a great chance for more conversation.

Example Sentences:
1) Can I help you clear the table?
2) Can I help you with the dishes?
3) Can I dry the dishes for you?
4) Can I do anything to help?

Example Conversations:
1)
Satoshi: Can I do anything to help?
Diane: Oh, that's very kind of you Satoshi. Jane will wash the dishes. Could you dry them for her?
Satoshi: Sure. I'd be glad to. Where is the towel?

2)
Satoshi: Can I do anything to help?
Diane: Oh, that's very kind of you Satoshi, but it is OK. Our children do the washing and cleaning after meals. You go into the living room and relax. There is a good TV show coming on soon.
Satoshi: OK, thank you.

COFFEE BREAK

Remember, it is a cultural experience for the host family too, so why not take some ingredients from your country and cook them a traditional dish?

We recommend our students do this, and the host family has always been delighted. One student from Japan made okonomiyaki pancakes. Another student took matcha green tea powder, a tea whisk, tea bowls and traditional Japanese sweets. She did a small tea ceremony, and when she finished, she gave the bowls as presents. The host family loved it!

Here are some sentences you can use
1) Would it be OK if I cooked one night? I'd like to make you some home cooking from my country.
2) Would you like to try my mother's noodle recipe?
3) Could you show me how to use the oven/gas range/stove/microwave please?
4) I have most of the ingredients*, but I need to buy some things. Next time you go to the supermarket, could I go with you please?
5) Where do you keep the wooden spoons/pans/knives?

** **Be careful!** Check if you can take the ingredients into the country before you go.*

10. DAILY CONVERSATION

Q. Please tell me some useful phrases I can use to talk about daily life.

Here are some useful phrases and example conversations, which you can use with your host family.

Mornings
Example Sentences:
1) What are your plans for today?
2) What are your plans for the weekend?
3) Could you pick me up around three pm, please?
4) I can catch the bus home. Is there a bus stop near the school?
5) I think I'll go shopping after school. I will catch the bus around five pm. Is that OK with you?
6) I can walk home. It isn't far.
7) I will call you/message you if I get lost.
8) We are going on a trip to London, so I won't be back until seven o'clock.
9) Are there any buses at that time?
10) After school I'm going for dinner with some of the other students.

Example Conversation:
Diane: Good morning. Did you sleep well?
Satoshi: Yes, thank you. I slept very well. How about you?
Diane: Very well, thank you. What are your plans for today?

Satoshi: My first class starts at nine o'clock, and I finish school at three pm.

Diane: How are you getting home? Shall I pick you up?

Satoshi: That's very kind of you, thank you. Where should I wait for you?

Diane: Wait outside the main entrance of the school. I will be there just after three.

Satoshi: OK, thank you.

Evenings

The host family will want to know about your day, and you should ask them about their day too.

If they ask you how your day was, remember to add some extra information.

Answer+ and Answer ++.

Example Conversations

1)

John: How was your day?

Satoshi: It was good. We had a conversation class. I was in a group with students from Korea, Egypt and Russia. Everyone was really nice. I had a great time, and I learnt a lot about their countries.

John: That sounds good. I'm glad you enjoyed your day.

Satoshi: How about you?

John: I had a busy day. I had meetings at work, and then I had to go to the next city to pick up some documents.

2)

John: What are your plans for the weekend?

Satoshi: I don't have any plans. How about you?

John: We are going to the supermarket on Saturday morning.

Satoshi: Would it be OK if I came too?

John: Sure. We can have lunch at a café near the supermarket, and then, if the weather is nice, we can go for a drive.

Satoshi: That sounds great, thank you.

11. INSTRUCTIONS AND DIRECTIONS

Q. *I have to take the bus to and from school every day. How do I use the bus? Will it be the same as my home country?*

Advice: The ways of using public transport are different depending on the country. You should ask your host family how to get to and from their house. Use the example sentences below.

Example Sentences:

1) Could you teach me how to use the bus? Do I pay when I get on or when I get off?
2) Where is the nearest bus stop?
3) What is the bus stop near the school called?
4) When I get on the bus to come home, what should I say to the driver?
5) Where is the nearest taxi stand?
6) Can you tell me the phone number of a taxi company?
7) Could you call a taxi for me please?
8) Can I buy a train ticket at a machine, or must I go to the counter?
9) What is the name of the nearest train stop?
10) Could you tell me how to get from your house to the school please?
11) Could you show me your house on this map please?
12) Could you tell me your address?

Example Conversation:

Satoshi: Could you tell me how to use the bus please? I'm going to come home by bus tonight.

John: Sure. Get on through the front door, and tell the driver the name of your stop. He will tell you how much to pay. Give him the fare, and take your ticket. It's easy!

Satoshi: What is the name of the nearest stop?

John: The nearest stop is called Berkshire Road. Just say 'To Berkshire Road please'. The driver will understand.

Satoshi: Could you tell me how to get from the bus stop to your house?

John: Yes, it's very near. Get off the bus and take the first right, then the first left. You will see our house on the right.

Satoshi: That's great, thanks. Can you tell me your address just in case I get lost?

John: It's 14 West Drive. But I'm sure you won't get lost.

Satoshi: Thank you very much!

12. PRESENTS

Q. I want to take some presents for my host family. What should I take?

Advice: We are sure your host family will be very happy to receive anything from you. Something traditional from your country is a good idea. But don't take anything too big, heavy or expensive! Our Japanese students have taken many things, such as chopsticks, fans, tea bowls, lacquerware, T shirts, manga, dolls, postcards of their hometown, sweets, green tea, tea pots, vases…

Here is an example of Satoshi giving his host family presents.
Example Conversation:
Satoshi: Do you have free time now?
John: Yes, we do.
Satoshi: I have some presents for you from Japan.
John: Oh thank you!
Satoshi: This is for you. I hope you will like it.
John: Oh, a Japanese baseball cap! This is wonderful. Thank you!
Satoshi: And this is for you Diane.
Diane: A fan! This is really pretty!
Satoshi: I'm glad you like them. I brought you some Japanese cookies and some green tea too. The cookies are sweet potato flavour.
Diane: They sound delicious. Thank you. Let's open them.

COFFEE BREAK

"When Naomi was staying with us, my mother had her eightieth birthday. We had a party for her. Naomi bought her a card and a bunch of flowers. She was so pleased! I was pleased too. It felt like she was a member of the family."
Host father to a student from Japan

"I love sport. My host family liked sport too. I was very lucky. They took me to a football match. One of the players was from my country. It was a special experience. Usually I don't have the chance to see high level football games. The atmosphere was amazing! I'm sure the ticket to the football match was very expensive. When I returned to my country, I sent my host father and mother a cap and a flag of my local football team as a thank you present. They were delighted!"
Mr J.H. (21) Visited the UK

13. SICKNESS AND ACCIDENTS

Q. If I feel unwell, or if I have an accident, how can I tell my host family?

Advice: If you feel unwell, or if you have an accident, you should always tell your host family. They will be able to take you to a pharmacy or the hospital. Here are some useful sentences.

Example Sentences:
1) I don't feel very well.
2) I think I am getting a cold.
3) Do you have a thermometer I could use, please? I think I have a fever.
4) I have a sore throat. Could you take me to the pharmacy to buy some medicine?
5) I have a headache. I'd like to buy some painkillers.
6) I fell down the stairs at school and hurt my foot. I can't walk very well.
7) I think I need to see a doctor.
8) I cut my hand when I was slicing the bread this morning. Do you have a plaster and some antiseptic?
9) I have a bad stomach.

Example Conversation:
Satoshi: I don't feel very well.
Diane: Oh, really? What's the matter?

Satoshi: I have a bad stomach and a headache. I think I might have a fever too. Could you take me to the pharmacy so I can buy some medicine?

Diane: We have some medicine here. I will go and get it. If you need more medicine I can go to the pharmacy for you. You should go to bed and have a rest.

Satoshi: Thank you. I think I might be getting a cold.

Diane: I hope not. You should have an early night tonight. If you don't feel better tomorrow morning, we can take you to the doctors.

Satoshi: Thank you. I think I will take a rest in my room.

Diane: OK, I'll bring the medicine and some water up to you.

14. SAYING GOODBYE

Q. How should I say goodbye?
Advice: It depends on the family and on you, but in our experience, many host families and students become close. Some students and host families cry at the airport because they are so sad to say goodbye. Some hug, some shake hands, some just say goodbye. There is no right answer. Do what is natural for you at the time.

Example Sentences:
1) I had a really wonderful time with you.
2) Thank you for letting me stay with you.
3) I hope we can keep in touch.
4) I hope we can see each other again someday.
5) Are you on Facebook? I'll send you a friend request.
6) Do you use Twitter?
7) I'll send you an email when I get back.
8) I will miss you.
9) Thank you for everything.
10) Please keep in touch.
11) I will write soon.

Example Conversation:
Satoshi: Thank you for letting me stay with you. I had a wonderful time.
Diane: We had a wonderful time too. We are glad you enjoyed your time with us.

Satoshi: Are you on Facebook?

Diane: Yes, we are.

Satoshi: Can I send you a friend request?

Diane: Yes, please do! We would love to stay in touch with you.

Satoshi: I hope we can see each other again someday. Please come to Japan. You can stay with my family!

John: Thank you! That would be great! I've always wanted to go to Japan!

Diane: Have a safe trip back home. Email us when you get back.

Satoshi: I will. Thanks again! Bye!

Diane and John: Bye!

THANK YOU

Thank you for reading Enjoy Your Homestay. (Word count: 7,477) We hope you enjoyed it, and we hope you enjoy your homestay too!

If you would like to read more about homestays, please see our Level 1 graded reader "A Homestay in Auckland".

If you would like to read more graded readers, please visit our website http://www.italkyoutalk.com

Other Level 3 graded readers include
A Dangerous Weekend
A Holiday to Remember
Akiko and Amy Part 1
Akiko and Amy Part 2
Akiko and Amy Part 3
Be My Valentine
Different Seas
Enjoy Your Business Trip
I Need a Friend
Old Jack's Ghost Stories from England (1)
Old Jack's Ghost Stories from England (2)
Old Jack's Ghost Stories from Ireland
Old Jack's Ghost Stories from Japan
Old Jack's Ghost Stories from Scotland
Old Jack's Ghost Stories from Wales

Party Time!
Stories for Christmas
The Curse
Together Again
Who is Holly?

ABOUT THE AUTHOR

I Talk You Talk Press is a Japan-based publisher of language textbooks, graded readers and language learning/teaching resources.

Our team is made up of highly experienced language teachers and translators, who have all studied at least one additional language to an advanced level.

This experience enables us to design our materials from the perspective of both the teacher and the learner. We consult with both teachers and language learners when designing our textbooks and graded readers, and test our materials extensively in the classroom before publication.

We are a fast-growing press, and currently publish graded readers for learners of English. We publish new graded readers monthly.

www.ingramcontent.com/pod-product-compliance
Lightning Source LLC
Chambersburg PA
CBHW022345040426
42449CB00006B/721